T0346196

Welcome to Busy Book 6!

Can you find these things in the book? Write the page number in the star.

The Busy Book helps children develop in the following areas of learning...

 Communication
Learning to speak together in English.

 Leadership
Learning to build relationships.

 Discovery
Building knowledge and awareness of social responsibility.

 Critical thinking
Solving problems and puzzles and learning thinking skills.

 Creativity
Expressing ideas through drawing and making.

 Self-management
Learning to plan ahead to reach goals.

1 Let's stay healthy

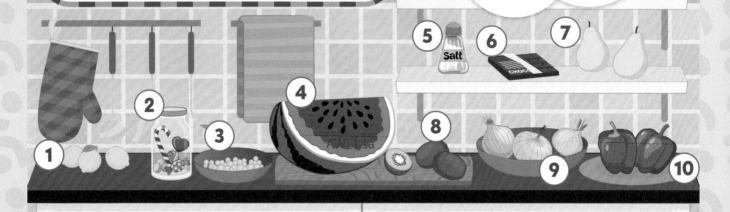

Order the letters to make food words. Then look, find and number.

I went to the kitchen and I found...

epar _____	☐
psae _____	☐
tals _____	☐
ikwi _____	☐
teswes _____	☐

lamtereown _____	☐
noion _____	☐
ecoclhaot _____	☐
mnelo _____	☐
epeprp _____	☐

Use the letters to make food words you know.

Word wheels

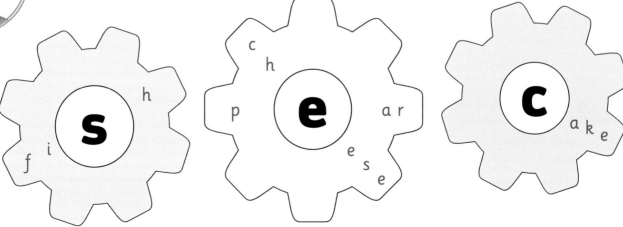

Su: Where did you go yesterday?

Omer: I went to the doctor. There was a long queue! I saw Sarah, Lola and Max there.

Su: Why did you go? What was the matter?

Omer: I had a cough and a temperature.

Su: Did you have a headache?

Omer: Yes, I had a bad headache too.

Su: Who did you see?

Omer: I saw Doctor Green – my favourite doctor! She told me to take some medicine, to rest and to drink a lot of water.

Su: Do you feel better now?

Omer: Yes, I feel much better today!

What's the matter? Write.

Sarah *I cut my finger!*

Lola _____

Max _____

You're the doctor! Ask questions.

? _____
_____

? _____
_____

? _____

? _____
_____

In other words

I went to the doctor.	I had a cough.	I played volleyball.	I did a puzzle.	I put on a show.
I ate a healthy breakfast.	I baked _____ .	I saw my friends.	I found _____ .	I took my sister to school.
I saw a cat in a tree.	I ate a healthy breakfast.	I cut some cheese.	I saw my teacher at the market.	I went to _____ .
I made _____ .	I saw _____ .	I ate a lot of sweets.	I had _____ .	I found my keys.

Tell a friend about yesterday without using the purple words.

Your sentence must start with 'In other words...'

Yesterday morning, there was a bowl of cereal, milk and fruit on my kitchen table.

Yes! I ate a healthy breakfast.

In other words, you ate a healthy breakfast.

Tongue twister

Can you say this five times quickly?

Peggy put the pepper on the paper.

Now make your own tongue twister!

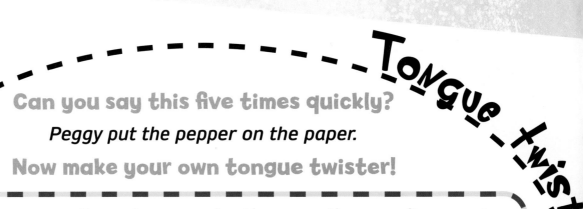

Ben   red   pens   yellow   lemons   brother   mother   waiter   water

_____

Our world

Add more foods to the list. Order them from 1 (your favourite) to 10 (your least favourite).

- ☐ curry
- ☐ sushi
- ☐ tacos
- ☐ yoghurt
- ☐ pizza
- ☐ _____
- ☐ _____
- ☐ _____
- ☐ _____
- ☐ _____

My favourite food is

_____.

It's from

_____.

When and where did you eat it? Who made it? Was it delicious? Draw.

I ate _____

at / in _____.

_____

_____

Do it yourself!

Smell test! Ask your family to give you four foods. Can you guess them by smell? Don't look!

I guessed:

1 _____ 2 _____ 3 _____ 4 _____

The correct foods were:

1 _____ 2 _____ 3 _____ 4 _____

I got _____ out of four correct!

My healthy habits journal

Circle and write before you go to bed.

Think about food, drink, activities, sports and medical advice.

	I feel...	What I did...
Day 1	well / ill	Today, I _____ and I _____.
Day 2	well / ill	Today, I _____ and I _____.
Day 3	well / ill	Today, I _____ and I _____.
Day 4	well / ill	Today, I _____ and I _____.
Day 5	well / ill	Today, I _____ and I _____.
Day 6	well / ill	Today, I _____ and I _____.
Day 7	well / ill	Today, I _____ and I _____.

Date: _____

I feel ☐ well ☐ ill.

What did you do to stay healthy this week?

_____

_____

_____

_____

_____

My favourite activity in this unit:

_____

Something new to try:

_____

Something I will remember from this unit:

_____

Let's be green

Level 1: Circle the things that are <u>hard</u> (darh) **not** <u>soft</u> (tofs). Put them in the puzzle.

| s | c | r | e | e | n |

sushi   gloves   (screen)   blanket   torch   key

Level 2: These things are <u>tiny</u> (yint) **not** _____ (eralg). Put them in the puzzle.

mouse   wolf   cabin   pea   taxi   coin

Level 3: Look and write. Then find things that are _____ (epmyt) **not** _____ (lulf). Put them in the puzzle.

<u>backpack</u>

<u>b_____</u>

<u>pl_____</u>

<u>g_____</u>

<u>su_____</u>

<u>b_____</u>

QUICK QUIZ

Which is messier? ☐ my bedroom ☐ my kitchen

Which is tidier? ☐ my classroom ☐ my street

The lightest room in my house is the _____.

The darkest month of the year in my country is _____.

Murat

Fatima

Fatima and Murat want to travel around the world. Read and choose.

'Shall we go to Predjama Castle in Slovenia?' asked Fatima. 'Look at its picturesque towers. It's the largest, most ancient castle in a cave.'

'Or... somewhere more modern? Hong Kong has the most skyscrapers in the world!' said Murat.

'I'm not sure, Murat,' said Fatima. 'I want to visit the Schönbrunn Palace in Austria. It is one of the most traditional palaces in Europe.'

Murat was excited. 'This looks more fun, Fatima! Xcaret is in an eco-friendly park in Mexico.'

Fatima smiled. 'Let's choose the most interesting place and go!'

Hi _____,

Today we went to _____ because

it's the most _____.

It's more _____ than _____.

Tomorrow we're going to _____.

_____

From Fatima and Murat

Write a postcard from Fatima and Murat.

Find out more about ancient castles around the world!

What am I thinking of?

Ask a friend. Write their answers here.

Write the first answer you think of.

		Me	My friend
1	It's a fruit that's large enough to use as a football.		
2	It's a sport that isn't interesting enough.		
3	It's an animal that's too dangerous to keep as a pet.		
4	It's something that isn't soft enough to sleep on.		
5	It's an activity you're too nervous to do.		
6	It's a room in your house that's too messy.		
7	It's a band or singer that isn't modern enough.		
8	It's an activity that's exciting enough to do on your birthday.		
9	It's a _____ that's _____ enough to _____ .		
10	It's a _____ .		

Count how many of your answers are the same as your friend's.

0	That's OK. Often, opposites make amazing friends!
1–4	Nice, it's good to have different ideas sometimes.
5–8	You make a great team!
9–10	Wow, you two sound like the same person!

CODE CRACKER

What is Julia's favourite food?

I like to eat a lot of different foods. I think chocolate is too sweet but kiwis are not sweet enough.

a=26, b=25 ➡ y=2, z=1

8 7 9 26 4 25 22 9 9 18 22 8

Our world

Theme parks use a lot of energy. But did you know that they can be eco-friendly? At GreenWood Family Park in the UK, the Green Dragon rollercoaster uses energy from the people waiting in the queue!

SolarSplash, a water ride, is the first solar-powered ride in the UK. The solar panels provide 80% of the park's energy.

Over 500 trees are planted at GreenWood every year. Trees collect carbon dioxide and make oxygen, which keeps the air healthy and clean.

Design a ride for a theme park using a wind turbine. Why is it eco-friendly?

_____
_____
_____
_____
_____

Do it yourself!

Tell your friends or family about your eco-friendly ride!

Explore your town or city.

What things do you see that use or make energy? Are they eco-friendly?

_____
_____
_____

My dream home journal

Read. Then draw and write about your dream home.

Would you like to live in a modern skyscraper? Or maybe an ancient tree house?

Is your dream home larger than your home now? Are the rooms full or empty?

Does it have solar panels or other eco-friendly designs?

My dream home

My favourite activity in this unit:

_____

Something new to try:

_____

Something I will remember from this unit:

_____

Ideas

Read the clues. Then write the words.

1 It floats in the sky and makes rain.

c l o u d
   11 4 13

2 It's a dark place inside a mountain.

___ ___ ___ ___
17 2   19

3 It's got seven colours.

___ ___ ___ ___ ___ ___ ___
20   7 1   12

4 Cows eat this green plant.

___ ___ ___ ___
10 5 9

5 It's a little river.

___ ___ ___ ___ ___
8 3   15

6 Plants grow in this.

___ ___ ___ ___ ___ ___
6 16   14 18

Use the numbers to answer the question.

Why are outdoor lessons popular in many countries?

Because   n   a   ___ ___ ___ ___   ___ ___ ___
      1 2 3 4 5 6   7 8 9

___ ___ ___ ___   ___ ___ ___ ___ ___ ___ ___ .
10 11 12 13   14 15 16 17 18 19 20

Use a mirror.

My nature walk

What was I doing __doing__ yesterday?

I was walking _____ along

the path _____ in the woods _____.

I was singing _____ my

favourite song.

Suddenly, I saw a huge

waterfall _____ in front

of me. It was amazing!

Write about something you were doing yesterday. Use words from this page.

_____

_____

_____

_____

There's a
thunderstorm tonight!
And there might be a tornado,
dangerous to everything in its path.
Let's stay safe and warm inside.

It's
a flood!
It was
raining all night
when the river got too
full and the water came in
my house. But there's a
drought in my friend's country.
It wasn't raining yesterday when
he looked outside the door.
And there's no rain
today.

The volcano
was sleeping when
we climbed it to the top.
I walked on the hungry giant under my feet.

Draw a natural world shape. Then write your own poem.

My poem

_____

_____

_____

_____

_____

_____

_____

13

The weather game

You have three minutes to look at the table.

00:00

Now choose.

City	Today	Tomorrow	Next week
Manchester, UK	🌡️	🌧️	☀️
Beijing, China	🌫️	☀️	🌡️
Chicago, USA	💨	☀️	🌧️
Santiago, Chile	🌡️	💨	🌧️
Venice, Italy	🌡️	🌫️	☀️

Level 1: you can remember one city.
Level 2: you can remember three cities.
Level 3: you can remember five cities.

Give the book to a friend.
They ask you questions.
How many did you get right?

Make your own table and test a friend!

What's the weather like in Manchester today?

It's cold!

City	Today	_____	_____
London, UK			
_____			
_____			
_____			
_____			

What's it going to be like tomorrow in Chicago?

It's going to be sunny!

?Riddle

I've got *fingers* and *songs* and *earrings*.
My special sound is
_____ ng _____.

I've got *watermelons* and *money* and *rain*.
My special sound is
_____.

Our world

What's the climate like where you live? Put a cross in the right place on each line.

temperature

cold   hot

hours of sunshine

few   many

snowfall

never   often

tornados

never   often

rainfall

a little   a lot

hurricanes

never   often

thunderstorms

never   often

Ask someone older than you to look at your chart.

Write their weather story.

What was the weather like when they were young?

Was it different? Are temperatures rising or falling?

_____**'s weather story**

_____ years ago, the weather was _____.

_____

Compared to today, the weather was _____.

_____

My weather journal

Draw yourself on TV.

You're on television! What's the important weather news?

Write.

BREAKING NEWS 09:26

Good morning!

Today, we bring you news of three extreme weather events from around the world.

Late yesterday night, everyone in the city of _____ was sleeping

when _____.

This morning, in _____,

there was a _____

_____.

Finally, _____

_____

_____

_____.

My favourite activity in this unit:

_____

Something new to try:

_____

Something I will remember from this unit:

_____

All about water

Look and write.

1

___comb___

2

_____

3

_____

4

_____

5

_____

6

_____

7

_____

8

_____

Change one letter to spell something in the bathroom. Write and draw.

1

___pink___ _____

2

___map___ _____

QUICK QUIZ

In the bathroom, I must _____ and

_____ but I mustn't _____

or _____ !

Finish the school newspaper.

Complete with time expressions like *on Tuesday* or *next month.*

The _____ News

Date: _____ 20 ____

Our water stars!

_____, the school Charity Club collected £500 for a water charity which provides safe, clean water. The charity builds water pumps and toilets.

_____, Olivia and Tymon gave the money to the head teacher in a huge bucket.
Well done, everyone!

In other news...

_____, two teachers found an ancient well under the playground!

_____, the teachers must make the well safe.

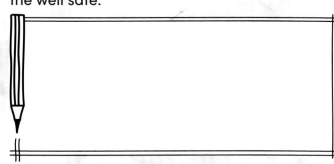

_____, there's going to be a Geography trip to the famous springs in Foggy Hills.

Mr Brown is going to send a letter about the trip to all parents _____.

BRAIN TEASER

Add three letters to make three connected words.

Clue: hair!

com ___ ru___ ___ ampoo

A to Z challenge

You can use the letter in any word.

Write requests using the coloured letters. Ask your family and friends. Tick or cross.

		✓ / ✗			✓ / ✗
a	_____?		n	Can I _____?	
b	Can I read your **b**ook, please?		o	_____?	
c	_____?		p	Could I have a **p**_____?	
d	Could I have a **d**rink, please?		q	Do you mind if I _____?	
e	_____?		r	_____?	
f	_____?		s	Can I **s**hare your _____?	
g	Do you mind if I _____?		t	_____?	
h	_____?		u	_____?	
i	Could I _____?		v	Do you mind if I play a **v**ideo game?	
j	_____?		w	_____?	
k	_____?		x	Can I _____?	
l	Do you mind if I **l**isten to the radio?		y	_____?	
m	_____?		z	Could I _____?	

Tongue twister

Can you say this five times quickly?

Sick Tim sits in the sink.   Five frightened friends fly.

Now make your own!

Philip   Lily   six   kick   big   picnic   biscuits   pink

_____

Our world

Complete the Water Quiz.

1 What should you clean in a washing machine?

- ☐ clothes
- ☐ plates
- ☐ your family

2 What should you change often in a fish tank?

- ☐ all the fish
- ☐ the water
- ☐ some rocks

3 Where do you usually find a dishwasher?

- ☐ in the bathroom
- ☐ in the garden
- ☐ in the kitchen

Now think of your own water question. Write and draw.

4 What should you flush in the bathroom?

- ☐ shower
- ☐ toilet
- ☐ toothbrush

5 _____ ?

- ☐ _____
- ☐ _____
- ☐ _____
- ☐ _____

Do it yourself!

00:00 How many ways can you find to save water in your house? You've got five minutes... Go!

bathroom: have shorter showers

_____

_____

_____

_____

Ask your family and friends to try the quiz!

My water journal

Tell the story of water.
Write and draw.

A LONG TIME AGO...

THEN...

THESE DAYS...

IN THE FUTURE...

IN THE YEAR 3000...

What did people drink in the past?

How did they wash?

What must we do to save water?

What mustn't we do?

What are bathrooms going to look like in the future?

My favourite activity in this unit:

Something new to try:

Something I will remember from this unit:

Can you talk about your journal for three minutes?

Look at the picture clues and write the correct job.

Jobs, jobs, jobs!

Complete the sentences.

I won't be a / an _____ or a / an _____.

I think I'll be a / an _____ or a / an _____.

My friend will be a / an _____ or a / an _____.

Imagine with Mateo

What will you do...?

Read, think and write words.

a school subject: ¹_____

a job: ²_____

a place of work: ³_____

clothes: ⁴_____ and

⁵_____

daily activities: ⁶_____ and

⁷_____

a food: ⁸_____

your friends: ⁹_____ and

¹⁰_____

two animals: ¹¹_____ and

¹²_____

two adjectives: ¹³_____ and

¹⁴_____

two numbers: ¹⁵_____ and

¹⁶_____

a country or city: ¹⁷_____

Now add your ideas to the story.

What will you do when you grow up? Will you like it?

When I grow up, I'll go to university to study ⁽¹⁾_____. Then I'll get a job as (a / an) ⁽²⁾_____ because I like working in / at the ⁽³⁾_____. I'll wear (a / an) ⁽⁴⁾_____ but I won't wear (a / an) ⁽⁵⁾_____. Every day, I'll ⁽⁶⁾_____ and ⁽⁷⁾_____. My favourite lunch will be ⁽⁸⁾_____.

I'll share a flat with ⁽⁹⁾_____ and ⁽¹⁰⁾_____. ⁽⁹⁾_____ will clean the flat and ⁽¹⁰⁾_____ will cook for us. We'll have a pet ⁽¹¹⁾_____ but we won't have a pet ⁽¹²⁾_____ because they're too ⁽¹³⁾_____!

After that, I'll have ⁽¹⁵⁾_____ ⁽¹⁴⁾_____ children. They'll start school when they're ⁽¹⁶⁾_____. I'll take them to ⁽¹⁷⁾_____ on holiday every year!

What will I do when I'm sixty? I'll _____ and I'll _____!

Find and write the blue letters hiding in the story. What job is it?

– – – – – – –

Clue: teeth

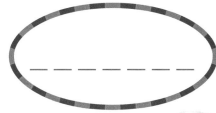

In the future...

> Think about what life might be like in the future.

Play with a friend. Write two ideas.

_____

_____

Now cover your notes. Play. Take turns to add your ideas.

> *In the future... we might have flying cars.*

> *In the future... we might have flying cars and we could go to university on the moon!*

> Keep adding more to the list! How many can you remember?

CODE CRACKER

What does Julia think will happen in the future? Use the code.

> *In 2099, I think we might...*

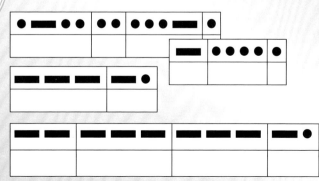

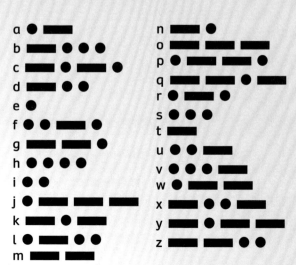

Our world

It's 'Explore Your Future' Day! Which jobs should these children try? Read and match.

Name: Alan

Likes: Languages, communication and writing.

Name: Matt

Likes: Maths, science and machines.

Name: Elena

Likes: History, reading and fixing problems.

I'm an engineer. I design buildings to be better for everyone, including disabled people.

I'm a lawyer. I support people at work. I check that they know their rights.

I'm a journalist. I interview people and write articles about equal rights.

Write and draw one more.

Name: _____

Likes: _____

_____

_____

I'm a _____.

_____

_____

_____

Do it yourself!

How many people do you know who work with food, animals, people or computers? Find out!

_____

_____

_____

My future journal

TOP SECRET

What job will you do?

I'll become a

_____

because

_____

_____

_____ .

Will you get a flat?

Yes, I will / No, I won't because

_____

_____

_____ .

To help create a fair world, I will...

1 _____

2 _____

3 _____

Will you have a pet?

Yes, I will / No, I won't because

_____

_____

_____ .

More 'future' notes:

My favourite activity in this unit:

_____

Something new to try:

_____

Something I will remember from this unit:

_____

> Find everything you need to complete your film!

START >>>>

SPIN AGAIN

> I haven't found a director yet.

Instructions

Play by yourself or work with a friend.

Spin the spinner to move.

If you land on a photo, say the word.

If you land on a speech bubble, say the sentence.

Keep going round until you've said all 10 film words.

MISS A TURN

> I've already found a camera operator.

SPIN AGAIN

> I've already found an actor.

What's my job?

Circle the letters you need to spell these jobs.

1 h o ⓐ l c l t o y r

2 w o d i o r e d c t o a r n

3 d c a b o m e r a l   l o y p e w r o a t o r o d

The other letters spell two special places for films:

_ _ _ _ _ _ _ _ _ _ _ _ _ _

_ _ _ _ _ _ _ _ _ _

Imagine with Mateo
Have you ever...?

Have you ever done something to make
the world a better place?

Answer the questions and add two more.

		Yes, I have.	No, I haven't.
1	Have you ever written a blog about an important issue?	☐ Yes, I have.	☐ No, I haven't.
2	Have you ever shared an inspiring message online?	☐ Yes, I have.	☐ No, I haven't.
3	Have you ever collected money for charity?	☐ Yes, I have.	☐ No, I haven't.
4	Have you ever volunteered for a community project?	☐ Yes, I have.	☐ No, I haven't.
5	Have you ever published a book?	☐ Yes, I have.	☐ No, I haven't.
6	Have you ever given a speech?	☐ Yes, I have.	☐ No, I haven't.
7	Have you ever made a documentary?	☐ Yes, I have.	☐ No, I haven't.
8	Have you ever appeared on television?	☐ Yes, I have.	☐ No, I haven't.
9	Have you ever _____ ?	☐ Yes, I have.	☐ No, I haven't.
10	_____ ?	☐ Yes, I have.	☐ No, I haven't.

Or why not try...

- making a film about an important issue.
- giving a speech at school about a community project.
- making money for a charity you care about.
- making a documentary about an inspiring person.

How many did you tick? Can you choose one to try in the future?

Remember: everyone has different skills and ideas! Write about yours:

I've already _____

but I haven't _____

_____ yet, and

I want to _____

in the future!

Let's write a film!

Choose one idea from each box. You can add your own.

 **Film topic**

four friends
a family
a pet dog
a famous actor
a blog writer

_____

Scene

an ancient castle
a modern skyscraper
a summer camp
a messy bedroom
a volcano

_____

Props

a lemon
some toothpaste
a towel
an onion
a script

_____

Use your ideas to plan your film with a friend.

It's about four friends.

First, they are in an ancient castle.

Then, they find a lemon.

Next...

Now take turns to write about the film.

Our film is about _____.

First, _____.

Next, _____.

Then, _____.

In the end, _____.

Our world

How to interview an inspiring person!

It's exciting to interview someone who has tried to make the world a better place! You can find out more about their message and how they share it with the world.

Try to ask questions for a long, interesting answer. You could ask:

- Who's responsible for looking after our world? Why?
- What's your most successful project?
- What do you do if a project is unsuccessful?
- Have you ever appeared on television?
- Did you feel more nervous or more excited?

responsible

inspiring

successful

Let's plan it!

Who do you want to interview? _____

What questions do you want to ask them?

1 _____

2 _____

3 _____

4 _____

5 _____

How can you inspire other people?

I can _____.

I've already _____ and I'd like to _____

_____.

My film journal

Plan your life story!

Interesting things I've done:

_____

_____

_____

_____

Actors:

-
-
-
-
-
-

Props:

Costumes:

_____

_____

_____

_____

_____

_____

Ideas:

First...

Then...

Next...

In the end...

Soundtrack: ♪♫♪

-
-
-
-
-
-
-

My favourite activity in this unit:

_____

Something new to try:

_____

Something I will remember from this unit:

_____

Goodbye

About me

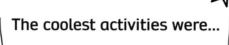

This book was...	The coolest activities were...	I'll tell my friends about...
_____ _____	_____ _____	_____ _____

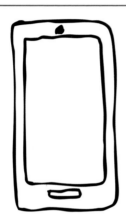  

Rise and Shine Certificate

You finished Busy Book 6!
Well done!

Awarded to: _____

Age: _____ Date: _____

Omer
Omer

Julia
Julia

Su
Su

Mateo
Mateo

Anita
Anita